The Purpose of Being

The Purpose of Being

Undra L. Ware Sr.

ISBN: 0998001201
ISBN 13: 9780998001203

Undra's Creation

Dedicated to my mother and father, Mary L. and Jimmy L. Ware.

A Growing Seed

As a seed, we are of an existence that is unaware of its origin. Truly, someday that seed will have its day to blossom and be watered with love.

As we travel through time, the seed becomes stronger and begins to bud from its roots. Now that the buds are growing from that seed from within, life will show that seed what will be and what was done.

Just as that seed has to grow, you as a person have that chance. The door has opened to a new lifestyle; your opportunity is here.

From a seed you are to an adult you will be, you must grow until your buds have blossomed to its fullest.

After all that has been done, you must then surpass life's richest treasures from that seed to the end.

What Is Life?

Life is an existence beyond imagination. The earth and its inhabitants are life. The richness of the dirt is life. So, as we can see, there was an existence of life before mankind was made.

We all know mankind was made of the dust and put into shape and form. So I say unto you, brothers and sisters, we are what we see. We are in a cycle that must be complete.

Life is a grand opportunity to live a prosperous victory in God's plan. Life is to see what is going on in this world and what is to come.

Life is a priceless experience, even though we are taxed at birth for food, clothing, housing, and work. We should enjoy life, because without life, we are of no existence.

How much is one life worth? Life is worth more than gold or precious stones, and we know, in this world, these things are expensive. We also know people kill and steal for minerals like these. So ask yourself: "Can I bring life back?"

They say only the strong survive. How is that so when we have many weak people? I feel if there is a strong one out in the crowd, he or she must be the chosen one to guide the weak and to feed them with spiritual knowledge.

What Is a Man?

Man is a male species composed of the earth's substance and is made to be strong, capable, and in control.

Do muscles make a man? A man doesn't have to be made of muscles. People seem to forget muscles are nothing but swollen tissue under layers of skin. What good are muscles if one can't solve today's worldly problems?

Being a man doesn't mean having women living in all four directions. Having all these women doesn't mean a thing but trouble. Maybe if you become surer about yourself, then you'll realize one is enough. Besides, if all these women had a child by you, how would you provide for them?

I've never seen a law saying, "A man should not have female characteristics." How can you change something that is genetic? I always thought if a man chose to be a woman, then it was a sin. When you think about it, you might as well say Jesus had female genes. He had love in his heart, he was caring and sensitive, he forgave the wrong and strengthened the righteous, and he had long hair and was soft spoken. Finally, he loved us so much that he died on the cross for us. But let's remember that this was a man.

In conclusion, I believe it's what on the inside that matters. A man should have courage and be strong, have a sense of direction, take charge, show leadership and quality in what he does, and not be racist.

The Black Man

Where shall we go, and whom shall we run to? Black men are victims of circumstances. We are under graded, segregated, and unappreciated.

I sympathize with the brothers that are struggling in this cruel racist world. We were taught to be honest and trustworthy. For what? Why should we smile and hold back our grudges while getting stabbed in the back. We are too smart to be fools. A brother without qualifications doesn't mean a thing in this society because we are black and cannot grow. The Constitution mentions "equality," but where is it?

The white man says that there is no more slavery, but working for the white man and not getting compensated for it, is like still being in slavery. How can we grow if we are not being tried?

What really makes us look bad is that they give opportunities to the sisters because they are claimed to be the weaker sex. So, sisters, let's be realistic; all brothers are not as bad as they seem. A brother can only take so much; being a minority is saying, "We really don't need you, but we'll see what we can do."

Sisters, I say to you, "Understand the brother, for without you, we are nothing." Some men don't know it, or they won't admit it. You are the road and the passage for us. Always remember where you come from and where you are going. If we don't stick together, how will we ever make it? Until I die, I will always know there's nothing like a helping hand from one another.

Black Butterfly

We as the black butterfly must teach our generations about the struggle for freedom we've surpassed, not only for the past generation but also for the present and future as well.

The children must know it was our dreams that cultivated our faith and brought us through desolation. Now that we are free, let's teach the children to move forward, to be seen and be heard.

We as God's children have the light; we just have to open our minds and eyes because we are too close to glory.

So let us all remember that whenever we need it, we can always go back and read it, for God is with us forevermore.

A Dream

A dream is a person's deepest thought from within, which he or she hopes to fulfill someday. A dream is something no man can take away from you unless he is God, the creator.

Those who dream, but of good dreams, and believe in themselves, they shall bring forth their dreams. A dream is a visualized picture of what a man or woman has accomplished or failed at.

If your heart and mind are right, your dream and desire to succeed will arrive within due time. I close by saying, "Keep dreaming, my child; without a dream we become nobody, but as long as you are dreaming, you have something to strive for." No one will give it to you, and it is dishonest to take it.

The key to life is to strive and earn whatever it is in life that you want. We came a mighty long way, and God knows we are too close to stop now. What you can't see now will appear to you later.

Dreams and Visions

In the night hours while in your deepest thoughts, all of a sudden you experience a reformation of the body. My spirit leads my body on a journey—a journey of my life situations and reactions. Even as I stand still, I know there is another in my soul. I feel there is a spiritual duel on the inside between good and evil. I know there is one of me, but there seem to be two others. I see myself in the middle while they are discussing what will be done. The thought of all this really scares me, for I know not what will happen.

To see a loved one get hurt by me makes me ache because I don't have an understanding of what's going on. But whichever emotion is stronger, that is the one that dominates and controls the mind.

I have experienced hatred and love. I realize when I think of hatred, it will destroy and become violent with thoughts of destruction. Love is more settled, caring, and open.

The most beautiful dream I had was the mountaintop. The mountain was so high and wide that there was enough room for many people, and it was very peaceful and free up there. I heard a voice asking, "Would you like to go down?"

I replied, "No. If I have to fall, I'd rather find another way."

The second voice stated, "I want to go down." My thought was that he was crazy. But whatever it was, it looked like a spiritual form going down in a red sled.

I even had a vision about being on trial by an unseen voice. The vision was only of me sitting in a pew and being surrounded by empty benches. No one in the jury or on the bench. A voice stated, "I have a gift." Next, it said, "I have been chosen." Finally, the voice spoke of going and telling people...I never got the rest of the message, but I have a feeling of what it might be. The question is, am I ready? But during that experience, everything that was said to me was so real, I awakened from my sleep, telling all of it to my spouse, as if she were a witness.

There was a time I use to wonder what it was that Dr. King saw. I know now that the King lives in me, and God is my savior, for I have seen the mountaintop, and I have been tried. I will have to overcome my fears and stand tall, for God is giving me revelations. I must walk on until that big day and always remember that I am somebody.

The Truth of the Light

Who can withstand the light? Where and when shall it shine upon you? Will you stand tall and speak fearlessly?

To stand tall in the light is true power that no man can endure. Many times, you will stand alone, but you must be strong for the journey ahead. Our people fail to realize that there is so much depression because there is not enough confession to see such a great transgression.

I believe if all nations start confessing to all these errors, innocent people won't be in such a great depression, and every soul must be sincere about the transgression; then prosperity will reach throughout the land.

When you think about it, this is a big world full of people. Since this is our world, you would think we could take care of it as well as ourselves. After all, we all need each other; that's why we are here. Yet we still can't get along.

We need to conquer negative ways such as greed, selfishness, ignorance, and stubbornness. So I ask you, "Who can withstand the light? Who has the light?"

Potential Growth

March rain adds moisture to the grain as April flowers begin to spring.

Each day grows longer as our anticipation of spring flows stronger.

Everyone seems to smile with ease when the warm air blows, which makes them well pleased.

This is the time for rejuvenation, and everyone follows their own dedication.

Since better days are growing near, let's dilute our fears and open our hearts to show that humans can care.

A Birthday for You

Today is your birthday; you should smile with complete joy. Another year of growth is granted to you.

The blessing of another birthday is a gift within itself to expand world knowledge.

This day has granted you another day of love, which will strengthen you through the years;

a week of knowledge to explore and understand the mystery of life; and a month of wisdom to teach the unwise and pray that nothing can take it away.

In the end, life itself will reward you for hanging through the hardships. The strength you earned will be yours forevermore, and the good times you will truly remember.

So I say to you, "Always be grateful for this day because it's yours to have, and it's your birthday."

The Strength

Before man came into existence, there was dust; now that man has power and authority, he has learned to lust.

Power should be used as a tool and not be given to a man-made fool.

Power should go to the one who truly deserves as long as the moral values of life are well preserved.

Power is very extravagant, and it brings about its own prosperity whether it's used for selfish gain or creating various pain.

Power will always live throughout the human race, so let's put it to use and pray for grace.

The Power Source

Myself:

I see myself as a member of the royal family—a very high-and-mighty, glorious, and victorious family.

I have a light that glows and shines ever divinely. For my father gave me the love and the mind to become whatever's in my will.

I hold power and glory in my heart, mind, and soul. So behold—look at all my achievements and goals.

As you can see, I am the child of a true and living God.

Christmas

Christmas is a day of rejoicing, giving, caring, and believing. Christmas is the day the savior was born, and on this day our salvation began.

This day is for joy, peace, happiness, and giving of good tidings. Family and friends share another joyous holiday that flows with harmonious love.

I see the spirit of Christmas flowing with love throughout cities, states, and countries. This is a day of peace and togetherness, not of war and despair.

As the spirit touches every living soul, we should always remember that Christmas should be in our hearts every day. The spirit of love shouldn't only be remembered on the day of December 25. If you believe it's real, then there will be peace on earth.

Happy New Year

A New Year's cheer is to bring in the new and
dispose of the old.

A much better perspective in the future plans another
challenge that is in demand.

A goal that is created to be reached, self-determination is
used until it is complete.

Another year for the unexpected, grief and joy as well as
pain, another year to experience higher planes.

Each year has its own gain, and not one stays the same.
As we celebrate this New Year, let's bring it in with a
great cheer.

The eighties had its blast, and the nineties are coming very
fast. We close out the year by putting it to rest and look
forward to the best.

Happy New Year!

King Greeting Card

As we come near this special day, we come to say thanks in our own God-giving way.

Thanks for the dream of equality, for now we can stand as one among ourselves and walk together as a people.

Thanks for the march on Washington that's instilled in our hearts and made its mark for freedom.

Let's thank God for this spiritual leader who's now laid down to rest as his job and his words still linger.

In the end, we all know that the King Dream will always ring, for the light is forever shining.

The Quest of Black History

Black history is a library that consumes all our black Americans who contributed many great achievements in their life-span.

These significant men and women died and left a future plan; it is we, the future, who have the upper hand.

It was our ancestors who wore the chains of slavery and endured the affliction of pain so that someday their future children would enjoy a much higher plane.

As black people, God has given us power to overcome, so look back, and observe all that has been done.

So let's keep in mind; black history is for us to cherish and teach our children, so it will not perish.

For many, history may repeat itself, but there is room for additions. So, remember, live to be the best, as our great ones lay down to rest.

Love and peace to all.

Happy Birthday Mom

A mother's love is something to cherish; my mind and heart make it hard to perish.

Throughout the years of screaming, teaching, and preaching, your hard labor is well overdue. Now is my turn to do for you.

I have little money, but I do have grace, and I will share this with you in any place.

As you can see, I am a part of you and what you made me, and these inspiring words are to say, "Happy Birthday" in my own special way.

The love you gave was always praised, and my love is natural, and that you should know; it's not often said but as you read, it shows in the flow.

Happy B-day from your number one, and remember, it is a blessing to be your son.

An Easter Miracle

An Easter treat that can't be beat and my eyes didn't deceive me. God revealed a sign of true rebirth as I captured nature at its best.

Dark clouds moved in from north to south and covered the heavy gray fog over the lake. Rain showers began to fall, but it didn't last long because of a call.

In a blink of an eye, there was a new day; the sun had shone from west to east as if the Lord was at peace.

A rainbow appeared in the sky like a miracle right before my eyes. Its connection to both ends of the lake made it believable and not a mistake. Its red, yellow, pink, orange, and blue colors were something to behold; now I know it's the master who created the mold.

The lake was calm and shaded with brightness as God rose in its likeness.

A Graduation for Brother

A graduation just for you, I hope all your dreams come true. The sense of success is in your hands; the power of the mind creates a plan. Graduation is the beginning of new challenges far ahead, and only a strong mind and heart will spread. As we celebrate this great day, I hope your intellect grows in the right way.

What you need is **Guidance** to succeed.
Respect for the ignorance and the less knowledgeable.
A positive **Attitude** to reach the right altitude.
Be **Decisive** about opportunities and obligations.
Understand one's self and needs.
Appreciate what and who you are.
Talent is to be used internally and externally.
An **Incentive** to be the best.
Keep an **Open** mind for various options.
Never say no to possibilities.

Success has no obligation, but the person who seeks must find the location. So, you can have it your way, and enjoy your graduation day.

Devotion

Devotion is a past and present form of dedication to any and every situation.

It's a matter of strength and determination.

This is the mark of a new beginning of trust and faith, keeping the foundation of love.

The courage and willpower to withstand temptation and to build hope in future affairs.

Through it all, the love that is bonded will triumph over one's flaws, and in the end, the promise of joy will shine upon us all.

Then you will know that through it all the power of devotion will always stand tall.

A Splint Heart

A splint heart is like a subtle wound that can easily
be infected.

An infection that has its resurrection and can be
cured by a love inspection, which will dispose or
release the drug injection.

A splint that is small in heart, oh how this hurt…
just don't depart. This tiny object that I can feel lets
me know that the pain is real. I just pray every day
for it to heal.

The heart is a victim of such an object; maybe time
will reject and sow the subject.

The heart is strong and very insecure; this is what
makes us unsure.

When the splint shall fall no one knows or cares,
but it is the heart that bonds and draws near.

Death

When death calls, it brings sorrow to our heart. Instead of rejoicing, it brings tears of mourning to see a beloved one lying down in their resting bed carefree of their life's troubles and miseries.

We seem to forget God is in control now. For this is the homecoming from the world's battle. I know it's hard to let go physically and mentally, but spiritually that person will still be with us. Even though we can't see them, the memories will always be cherished.

So let us not mope, for death is a calling for peace, not of the world's miseries and pain.

Though death springs upon us unannounced, it will either make us stronger or devastate us. But hold your woes, for nothing is dead; our body is the matter of the earth. We must always remember that the soul will always live on.

Gray Thursday

A deep sadness is in my heart as reality departs from my soul.

My inner thoughts form a big hole that rarely shows, and nobody knows the emptiness that is sought.

The things in my life seem to be a mistake, and sometimes I sit and mope as my body aches.

My life for now is a bit distressed, and my anger and hostility brings about unrest.

One day I will rise and fly like a human bird in the sky, as I await my wings and the bells of freedom to ring.

Relieving of Pain

Pain is a buildup of hurt that no human being can escape.

The strength of endurance is our only hope.

Prayer is our only answer. A sincere heart will deliver you over mountains, and the light will see you through darkness.

Our tears relieve the tension that flows through our mind and heart.

A human being may not always understand, but a child of God knows. So weep not, and be strong because in the end, we will win.

Workforce

Today there is a task to work together as one.

The challenge is more daring, and the days are much longer.

As we analyze each personality and overcome our conflicts, we become stronger.

The force is among us; it is we that must bring it forth.

How to Be a Winner

We as humans have an ultimate goal, a goal that puts us
above average and not less than the expected.

We strive every day to reach our specific peak, but some
fall short.

An individual must first have the desire to succeed.

Second, you must believe it is possible.

Patience will be an endurance of the mind,
heart, and soul.

Finally, all winners have the strength and courage that
triumph them to victory.

Survivor

For many, tragedy comes in different ways, no matter what hour
or time of day.

God has granted you life once more, so be thankful it is you he
truly adores.

Life could have been ended without a thought, but when the light
shone, it was you that it sought.

Your job on earth is not complete, so spread the word among
those you meet.

God is good, and that you should know; it is your presence that
he had to show.

So keep the strength, as your faith grows every day as many
prayers go your way.

Jamaica Man

A real Jamaican stands tall and true; their pride and spirit guides them through.

Their island is the foundation that brings peace and rest; that is why I find it to be the best.

Golden Seas is a nice place to be; I urge all people to come and see.

The ocean roars in the night, but the calm waves keep you from being uptight. I see a few vultures soaring through the day—a nice piece of scenery, I must say.

The clear-blue sky seems to be forever, and the blue-green water flows so smoothly that it soothes me.

With a vision to end, I see light rain showers that brighten the various flowers. To the Golden Seas workers, I am well pleased because you made me feel at ease.

Peace!

Made in the USA
Lexington, KY
30 December 2017